SEVEN IMPERATIVES

SERVANTS OF CHRIST

Exploring The Bible

The cover image is taken from a Russian Orthodox Ikon of the 19th Century.

ISBN: 979-8-35091-526-6

Dedicated to Terry Sanford Smith

Table of Contents

FOREWORD

For some time, I have been rising every morning, prostrating myself on the floor, and praying the seven imperatives spotlighted in SEVEN IMPERATIVES to God. This is not a method, but it is a great help. Since I am in an intimate relationship with the Father of the Universe, I want to declare my intentions to heed each one of His imperatives. This process has been a game-changer for me.

The author explains how God wants us to keep the main thing the main thing so that our lives will be changed for the better. I have found that declaring God's imperatives first thing in the morning and the last thing at night penetrates my heart and transforms my behavior during the day.

We need a quiet revolution in this world. Those who can live these seven imperatives daily will become a part of a revolution that fills the world with inexpressible hope and indescribable love. Anxiety, fear, guilt, shame, hopelessness, and death are replaced by peace, freedom, forgiveness, immeasurable value, and a certain hope of resurrection.

Following these seven imperatives will help empower you to live the truth about your authentic self! The truth about you includes: "You have immeasurable value," "You are Loved," "You are not alone," "You are Forgiven," "You are Chosen," and "You are a Gift."

God has made it clear that we are all made in His image and are unique individuals, "fearfully and wonderfully made," who are known, loved, nurtured, and taught by God.

When practiced, these seven imperatives will lead you to become a "human work of art." You will be trained to celebrate being a human being, which is truly the greatest thing in the world.

Join me in this Quiet Revolution to live these imperatives that Moses and Jesus delivered long ago. They are a pathway to joy!

Dr. Terry S. Smith
Nashville, TN.

PREFACE

Decades ago, we came across the 34th chapter of Exodus (SHEMOT in Hebrew). That began somewhat of an obsession on our part to dig into the two verses that reveal God's ways most dramatically: Exodus 34:6-7. Many years later, a similar obsession is occurring over a handful of related verses in the first books of the Hebrew Scriptures. They outline key instructions about how to relate to the Creator of the Universe. Note that these verses are all in the imperative voice. They are not just "how to." They are emphatically "do!"

Written for Jewish disciples and published in Amsterdam around 1738, the *Mesillas Yesharim* makes an arresting assertion: *"When you examine the matter further, you will see that **true perfection is nothing other than cleaving** to [Hashem], blessed be He."* (Luzzatto's preface as translated into English in the Jaffa edition). The Hebrew word transliterated for cleaving is the word DEVEYKUS.

Though many of us have been studying the scriptures diligently for over forty years, we missed this special Hebrew word as well as the group of striking verses that either contain it or have other phraseology that imply a similar thought. These verses are all about how one should relate to our Creator. This short essay is a modest attempt to spotlight those verses. May we be ever faithful to Father in the following seven ways:

Love Him

Cleave to Him

Walk in His Ways

Keep His Commandments

Fear Him

Serve Him

Listen to His Voice

With regard to the Hebrew transliterations of the Masoretic Hebrew characters, please remember that Hebrew characters are written from right to left and read from right to left, whereas the transliterated words are read from left to right.

YOU AND GOD

Jesus is the Master at condensing the entire Biblical revelation into its essence. When a Scribe asked, "What commandment is foremost of all?", Jesus answered as recorded in Mark 12:29-31:

"The foremost is, *'HEAR, ISRAEL! THE LORD IS OUR GOD, THE LORD IS ONE; AND YOU SHALL **LOVE** THE LORD YOUR GOD WITH ALL YOUR HEART, AND WITH ALL YOUR SOUL, AND WITH ALL YOUR MIND, AND WITH ALL YOUR STRENGTH.'*

"The second is this: *'YOU SHALL **LOVE** YOUR NEIGHBOR AS YOURSELF.' There is no other commandment greater than these."* (see Deut. 6:5, Lev. 19:18, Mark 12:29-31).

In an encounter that Luke records with a Lawyer, the Lawyer asked what one must do to inherit eternal life and Jesus further condensed:

*"YOU SHALL **LOVE** THE LORD YOUR GOD WITH ALL YOUR HEART, AND WITH ALL YOUR SOUL, AND WITH ALL YOUR STRENGTH,*

AND WITH ALL YOUR MIND; AND YOUR NEIGHBOR AS YOURSELF."
(Luke 10:27)

It is always helpful to know what the main thing is and to keep the main thing the main thing! In the first six books of the Bible, we see that Father pulls together the most important aspects of our relationship to Him.

These statements are not along the lines of the Creator's proclamation of **His** ways in Exodus 34:6-7. There, the emphasis is on how **God** acts in His relationship with mankind and in particular with the Children of Abraham. From one point of view, Exodus 34:6-7 describes God's **WAYS** (what He does) as much as His character traits. In fact, most Jewish people resist thinking of God's self-revelation on Mt. Sinai as revealing character traits. Rabbi Maimonides said that God is so unknowable in terms of His nature that we can only know what we see Him do, that is, His ways. That will be important when you see how God wants us to relate to Him since several key verses emphasize our need to **Walk in His Ways**. The verses on which we focus are not about how He relates to us but **how He wants us to relate to Him**.

Our Heavenly Father spells out in Scripture the main features of how we should relate to Him because we need instruction. He spells out a game plan for how we may have a healthy relationship with Him by dividing ways to relate to Him into different categories. Each revelation in Deuteronomy is like a doctor's prescription to heal a sickness. Or like a pastor's or rabbi's recipe for how to relate for those that are married. It's not about what everybody else needs to do. **It is about what each one of us needs to do** in an intimate relationship with the Godhead. It's all about how to relate to our Creator.

Our Jewish friends have a way of looking at the world that is a bit different from that of a Christian. They see the entire universe like a Vestibule that prepares us for entering the "The World To Come," that is, for what Christians call Heaven. They believe the God of our Universe has designed the whole shooting match just for our preparation.

At first, that seemed a bit of a stretch, but as we muse about it, we see that Father has made us in His image, and our human capabilities are quite beyond comprehension. We are already peering into the absolute limits of the Universe and looking on a molecular level at things that are entirely invisible to the human eye. Our giftedness seems nearly unmeasurable. Look around you for proof: flying to Mars and beyond, seeing and speaking to people thousands of miles away, healing some of the most intractable diseases ever. Mankind is amazingly gifted to explore this universe in which we live. Every action we take, every discovery we make, prepares us in some way for what is to come. This includes times of adversity as well as times of joy.

The idea of the Universe as a Vestibule is a bit like the in-between world that C.S. Lewis imagines in *The Magician's Nephew*. Our time in the Vestibule is meant to prepare us for entering the World To Come. Seeing things that way points out how important it is, while we are in this dimension, to learn how to rightly relate to the One with whom we hope to join forever in the next—the one with whom we will delight and with whom we want to cleave throughout Eternity.

Seven verses found in the book of Deuteronomy (DEVARIM in Hebrew) and one in the book of Joshua (YEHOSHUA) offer deep insights into the nature of our relationship to Father, that is, what that relationship from our side should resemble. Let's look at the eight verses and see how they spell out where we should put our attention—what the main things should be for each one of us.

Deuteronomy 6:5

*"And you shall **love** the LORD your God with all your heart and with all your soul and with all your strength."*

   1. Love Him.

Deuteronomy 10:12-13

*"And now, Israel, what doth the LORD thy God require of thee, but to **fear** the LORD thy God, to **walk in all his ways**, and to **love** him, and to **serve** the LORD thy God with all thy heart and with all thy soul,*

*"To **keep the commandments** of the LORD, and his statutes, which I command thee this day for thy good."*

   1. Fear (Revere) Him.

   2. Walk in His Ways.

   3. Love Him.

   4. Serve Him.

   5. Keep His Commandments.

Deuteronomy 10:20

*"Thou shalt **fear** the LORD thy God; him shalt thou **serve**, and to him shalt thou **cleave**, and **swear** by his name."*

   1. Fear (Revere) Him

   2. Serve Him

   3. Cleave to Him

   4. Swear by Him

Deuteronomy 11:1

*"You shall therefore **love** the LORD your God, and always **keep** His directive, His statutes, His ordinances, and His commandments."*

1. Love Him.

2. Keep His Directives, Statutes, Ordinances and Commandments.

Deuteronomy 13:4

*"After the LORD your God shall ye **walk**, and Him shall ye **fear**, and His **commandments shall ye keep**, and unto **His voice shall ye hearken**, and Him shall ye **serve**, and unto Him shall ye **cleave**."*

1. Walk After Him.

2. Fear (Revere) Him.

3. Keep His Commands.

4. Listen (Obey) to His Voice.

5. Serve Him.

6. Cleave to Him.

Deuteronomy 19:9

*"if you carefully follow all of this commandment which I am commanding you today, to **love** the LORD your God, and to **walk in His ways** always...."*

1. Love Him

2. Walk in His Ways.

Deuteronomy 30:20

*"That thou mayest **love** the LORD thy God, and that thou mayest **obey his voice,** and that thou mayest **cleave** unto him: for he is thy life, and the length of thy days: that thou mayest dwell in the land which the LORD sware unto thy fathers, to Abraham, to Isaac, and to Jacob, to give them."*

1. Love Him.

2. Obey His voice.

3. Cleave to Him.

Joshua 22:5

*"But take diligent heed to do the commandment and the law, which Moses the servant of the LORD charged you, to **love** the LORD your God, and to **walk in all his ways**, and to **keep his commandments**, and to **cleave** unto him, and to **serve** him with all your heart and with all your soul."* (Joshua 22:5)

1. Love Him.

2. Walk in His Ways.

3. Keep His Commandments.

4. Cleave to Him.

5. Serve Him.

If we look at the instances that each category (Love, Walk in His Ways, etc.) occurs in the verses cited, we can deduce several important points.

SCRIPTURE	Deut. 6:5	Deut. 10:12-13	Deut. 10:20	Deut. 11:1	Deut. 13:4	Deut. 19:9	Deut. 30:20	Josh. 22:5	*Times*
Fear Him		x	x		x				3
Walk in His Ways		x			x	x		x	4
Love Him	x	x		x		x	x	x	6
Serve Him			x		x			x	3
Keep Commandmts		x		x	x			x	4
Cleave to Him		x	x		x		x	x	5
Swear by Him			x						1
Listen to His Voice					x		x		2
Instances	1	5	4	2	6	2	3	5	

Though the exact Hebrew structure may differ slightly in each imperative, you can quickly see three things from looking at the preceding chart. The first is that not one list is duplicated. I believe this is because each list contextually is making a special point applicable to the setting. Second, the word LOVE occurs more times (six) than any other just as Jesus would have predicted. The closely associated word **Cleave** occurs next in five scripture sections. **Walk in His Ways** and **Keep His Commandments** occur four times each; **Fear Him** and **Serve Him** occur three times; **Listen to His Voice** occurs twice and **Swear by Him** occurs once. Finally, the scripture with the most injunctions is Deuteronomy 13:4. These are not the only important imperatives in Scripture (for example, "Be Holy as I am Holy," Leviticus 20:26), but they are extremely important.

Let's look at these injunctions (verbs) in the order of their frequency in these eight texts.

LOVE HIM

דָּבַק

[THE ROOT IN
HEBREW IS AHAV]

To intimately love, to desire, to breathe after

Deuteronomy 6:5

*"And you shall **love** the LORD your God with all your heart and with all your soul and with all your strength."*

Luke 10:27

"And he answered, 'YOU SHALL **LOVE** THE LORD YOUR GOD WITH ALL YOUR HEART, AND WITH ALL YOUR SOUL, AND WITH ALL YOUR STRENGTH, AND WITH ALL YOUR MIND;'"

These two scriptures describe an all-encompassing Love for our Maker—a Father who, for our sake, directs us to open the entirety of our being toward Him. Our Love for God is called to encompass the entirety of our hearts, our Soul [NEPHESH in Hebrew, that is, our entire being], our strength, and our mind. Everything within us is called to action. The word for "all" modifies each division of the self. All-encompassing. All-consuming. Our highest good; our greatest affection, our deepest delight. We stir up this authentic love within ourselves, within our hearts, by recognizing what "great things he has done for us." (See 1 Samuel 12:24).

CLEAVE TO HIM

דָּבַק

[THE HEBREW ROOT IS DEVEYKUS]

To cling, cleave, adhere, stay with, catch by pursuit, stick to

*"If you delve into this matter further, you will see that the entire world was created for the use of man; the world in fact stands in great balance. For if man is drawn after the world and is distanced from his Creator, he becomes degraded and degrades the world with him. However, if he controls himself and **CLEAVES** [DEVEYKUS] to his Creator and uses the world only as an aid in the service of his Creator, he becomes elevated, and the world becomes elevated with him. For indeed, it is a great elevation for all things in creation when they are used to serve a spiritually perfected man.*

"When you examine the matter further, you will see that true perfection is nothing other than **CLEAVING** *to the LORD.... This is what King David means when he says in Psalm 73:28, "But as for me, closeness to God is my good...."* (*Mesillas Yesharim* (Path of the Just), Chapter One)

Important Scriptural References where the root word for cleave occurs:

"Therefore, shall a man leave his father and his mother, and shall **cleave** *unto his wife: and they shall be one flesh."* (Gen. 2:24)

"For if ye shall diligently keep all these commandments which I command you, to do them, to love the LORD your God, to walk in all his ways, and to **cleave** *unto him"* (Deut 11:22)

"But **cleave** *unto the LORD your God, as ye have done unto this day."* (Joshua 23:8)

"And they lifted up their voice and wept again: and Orpah kissed her mother-in-law; but Ruth **clave** *unto her."* (Ruth 1:14)

Surely, we want to focus on God's very personal word to us. Look at the very first time the underlying Hebrew word occurs in the Hebrew scriptures: Genesis 2:24. This is the term used to describe the cleaving to one's spouse in marriage after leaving one's parents.

There is no more intimate way to describe the closeness that the God of the Universe intends for us in our relationship to Him than the spousal example, and the word itself implies our need to move toward Him. It also is about not only our action but also our disposition and intention. The Hebrew concordances suggest that there is a sense of pursuit in the action of Cleaving. In other words, we are called to go after Him, to go after closeness, to go "hard after Him." May it be so!

WALK AFTER HIM

לָלֶכֶת בְּכָל־דְּרָכָיו

[THE HEBREW ROOTS
ARE YALAK KOL DEREK]

**To walk after or follow in a great variety of applications,
literally and figuratively**

We are also called to **Walk in all His Ways**. This calls to mind Moses's famous request of the Almighty after the Golden Calf episode, *"shew me now thy way."* (Exodus 33:13). There is little question that the answer to Moses's question is our famous Exodus 34:6-7 passage where God's ways are clearly revealed in words: *"...**compassionate** and **gracious, slow to anger** and **abundant in loving-kindness and truth**; preserving loving-kindness for thousands, **forgiving iniquity, rebellion, and sin**; yet He does not completely clear [of sin]. He visits the iniquity of parents on the children and children's children, to the third and fourth generations."* (Exodus 34:6-7; Rabbi

Rosenburg's translation). These "ways" are how we see God operate, that is, He walks in the Way of Compassion, the Way of Graciousness, and so forth.

We also see God's ways writ large in His dealings with humankind since the time of Adam as well as in the life of our Messiah, Jesus of Nazareth, Son and Anointed One. Jesus's interaction with God, with nature, and with people reveals how all those anointed with the Spirit of God are to act. When thinking of Sinai and Jesus, we should remember that Jesus declared that He WAS the Way, the Truth [EMETH in Hebrew], and the Light. (John 14:6). If we want to "walk after God," there is no better way than to follow how Jesus Himself walked.

All recorded historical encounters with the Almighty reveal how He walked and thus His ways. Since we are called to Walk in His Ways, we have plenty of historical examples for thoughtful meditation. Who better to mimic that the Lord of the Universe? Our little book, *WHO ARE YOU ANYWAY?*, focuses on His ways as revealed to Moses. Our prayer and hope is that God will gift us His ways as we lean into Him. Hebrew and the New Testament scriptures give us very specific examples, none higher than Jesus's declaration.

KEEP
HIS COMMANDMENTS

וּלְשֹׁמְרֵי מִצְוֹתָי

[THE HEBREW ROOTS
ARE SAMAR MITZVAT]

**Keep, observe, Celebrate,
Guard God's commandments, ordinances, precepts**

God's commandments are entirely for our benefit as the God of the Universe needs nothing. (See Irenaeus's *Against Heresies*). This means that every commandment is for our sake. They contain an almost exhaustive list of God's Operating Instructions. His injunctions never hurt us; they only help us. We can rejoice and celebrate that His kindness has been extended to our rational minds that we might be able to trust the boundaries contained in His Word for our protection.

When it comes to the call "Keep His commandments," there are three primary sections of Scripture. First, we have the Ten Commandments that were written on Mount Sinai. Here is a JPS translation from the Masoretic text of Exodus (SHEMOT) 20:3-17 as published in 1985:

1

You shall have no other gods besides Me.

2

*You shall not make for yourself a sculptured image, or any likeness of what is in the heavens above, or on the earth below, or in the waters under the earth. You shall not bow down to them or serve them. For I the Lord your God am an impassioned God, visiting the guilt of the parents upon the children, upon the third and upon the fourth generations of those who reject Me, but showing kindness to the thousandth generation of those who love Me and **keep My commandments**.*

3

You shall not swear falsely by the name of the Lord your God; for the Lord will not clear one who swears falsely by His name.

4

Remember the sabbath day and keep it holy. Six days you shall labor and do all your work, but the seventh day is a sabbath of the Lord your God: you shall not do any work—you, your son or daughter, your male or female slave, or your cattle, or the stranger who is within your settlements. For in six days the Lord made heaven and earth and sea, and all that is in them, and He rested on the seventh day; therefore the Lord blessed the sabbath day and hallowed it.

5

*Honor your father and your mother, that you may long endure on the land
that the Lord your God is assigning to you.*

6

You shall not murder.

7

You shall not commit adultery.

8

You shall not steal.

9

You shall not bear false witness against your neighbor.

10

*You shall not covet your neighbor's house: you shall not covet
your neighbor's wife, or his male or female slave, or his ox or his ass,
or anything that is your neighbor's.*

Second, these ten are included in the 613 commandments as articulated in the Oral Law that was codified by Maimonides 1108 years after the destruction of the Jewish Temple in Jerusalem. Each commandment is called a mitzva and all of them together, the Mitzvot. Every believing Jew hopes to carry out as many of these as possible during his or her lifetime to have a chance of entering into the *OLAM HABA*, the *World To Come*, but those on this side of God's sacrifice on the Cross have been freed from attaining a perfection that truthfully none of us could have obtained. However, the wisdom of God's commands and all of His injunctions still bring us true wisdom regarding how to live a good life in our current world **and** please our Creator.

A few examples of the 613 commandments give a good flavor of the remainder. 248 are considered positive commands (dos) and 365 are thought to be negative (don'ts). Just the first twenty underscore how helpful God's commands are from a very practical point of view.

To know there is a God. (Exodus 20:2).
To not entertain thoughts of any god beside Him. (Exodus 20:3).
To Love Him. (Deut. 6:4).
To fear Him. (Deut 6:5).
To sanctify His Name. (Lev. 22:32).
To not profane His Name. (Lev. 22:32).
To not destroy objects associated with His Name. (Deut. 12:4).
To listen to the prophet speaking His Name. (Deut. 18:15).
To not test the prophet unduly. (Deut. 6:16).
To emulate His ways. (Deut. 28:9).
To cleave to those who know Him. (Deut. 10:20).
To love other Jews. (Lev. 19:18).
To love converts. (Deut. 10:19).
Not to hate fellow Jews. (Lev. 19:17)
To reprove wrongdoers. (Lev. 19:17).
Not to embarrass others. (Lev. 19:17).
Not to oppress the weak. (Leviticus 22:21).
Not to gossip about others. (Leviticus 19:16).
Not to take revenge. (Leviticus 19:18).

The entire list includes instructions about how to relate to our Creator—how we should behave externally and be internally, what to do to be healthy physically, mentally, and spiritually, how our interpersonal relationships can thrive and be delivered from toxicity, what we should do and not do in our work and with our finances—each command outlines what our Jewish friends have tried to embrace as Best Practices. We want to live out our lives in such a way that God would say we have heeded His Word with great care. The injunction, *To **KEEP** [SAMAR] His Commandments*, puts the whole of the Bible into the category of a great treasure chest that is to be carefully stewarded, protected, guarded, and heeded. It is true that some of the 613 are applicable only to temple service. From a practical point of view, those are no longer practiced.

Third, we have Jesus's stunning amplifications of the Creator's Operating Instructions that are most extensively outlined in his Sermon on the Mount exposition as recorded in the Book of Matthew, Chapters 5-7. Most challenging perhaps is his emphasis on "turning the other cheek," loving one's enemies, and "going the extra mile." And we have His view that even a wayward glance may be the same as adultery.

These opportunities to heed God's heart for us are true treasures. Any true disciple wants to heed every "God tip" with all of his or her heart, soul, mind and strength. Nothing is done by rote; everything is to be done with joy and intention.

Our rabbinical friends underscore an important help in no longer tolerating our obsessions and personal actions that veer from God's clear instructions: the action of trembling. A Torah Scholar (one who gives his life to the study of the TORAH) is instructed that a proper response to even the slightest veering from the straight and narrow, a glance or a thought that begins to emerge that is off track, is to physically tremble. That is a great practical help to many, and may it be so to you.

FEAR/REVERE HIM

יָרֵא

[THE HEBREW ROOT
IS YIR'A]

To fear; morally to revere

Proverbs 9:10 says, *"The fear [YIR'A] of the LORD is the beginning of wisdom, and knowledge of the Holy One is understanding."* If fear or awe of God is the beginning of wisdom, then we need to embrace a deep dose of reverence.

We are called to be in awe of our Creator, to revere Him, to always recognize that we are relating to the Almighty One, the Creator of all the Universe. As C.S. Lewis has Mr. Beaver say of Aslan the Lion in *The Lion, The Witch and The Wardrobe*, *"Who said anything about safe? 'Course he isn't safe. But he's good. He's the King, I tell you."*

The willingness to Honor those in authority in the Western world is in short supply. Few people are inclined to show honor to anyone, much less those in authority. The lack of willingness to give honor where honor is due is a phenomenon that has been readily apparent for at least half a century. It takes determination to resist the drift of our current culture and learn to give authentic deference and honor to others, and show a healthy awe of those who are in authority. Fear of God is partially about the fact that He is the ultimate authority. If you find yourself continually bashing those in positions of authority, you are likely having trouble honoring the God of the Universe. Extending true honor requires seeing afresh those God has put in your life to both help and protect you.

Rabbeinu Yonah's nineteenth principle of reaching complete repentance is refraining from repeating a sin even though you have failed previously. Here, Rabbeinu Yonah encourages us to stir up our awareness of God's awesomeness and great power (in Hebrew, *YIRAS HAROMEMUS*), that is, the fear of the awesomeness of God and His great exaltedness. God helps us by allowing us to fear Him.

Deep worship of our Creator is a great boon. We are released into true awe when, lost to ourselves, we experience heartfelt times of worship. We are allowed to touch the *mysterium tremendum*, the awe inspiring mystery and majesty of Him who has brought us and the entire Universe into being. He loves us but is entirely Other. Worship brings us into a most helpful state.

We are called to be conscious on the one hand that we are in relationship with the most awesome Being imaginable while simultaneously Loving Him and Cleaving to Him. Recognition of *His* amazing pursuit of us, His selfless and costly gift of Himself, is like oil to the gears; it impels us to tightly adhere to the Godhead in spite of our unworthiness from a human point of view. Our unworthiness has been exchanged for His worthiness through the sacrificial gift at Calvary.

SERVE HIM

תַעַבְדוּ

[THE HEBREW ROOT
IS AVAD]

To serve, labor, do work

Has anyone ever asked you your vocation, your job description? Clearly, the Hebrew verb AVAD pinpoints that we are called to *work* for our Creator. In a true sense, it is our job description. *Serve, labor, work* for the Master—that sums it up. As the Apostle Paul put it, we have become God's Bond Slaves. We willfully serve as a bonded slave. *"...though he was in the form of God, did not count equality with God a thing to be grasped, but emptied himself by taking the form of a servant [DOULOS in Greek], being born in the likeness of men."* (Phil. 2:6-8). Paul is speaking of Jesus as a Bond Slave, one who gives himself up to another's will for service. We, too, are called to the service of God. In relationship to the Godhead, it is our job.

The prophet Samuel called the Israelites **to serve the Lord** *"in truth with all your heart."* (1 Samuel 12:24). May we serve Him authentically IN TRUTH, not in outward appearances of going through the motions but WITH ALL OUR HEARTS! Seriously consider whether, in truth, you are serving the LORD of the universe with a full heart. If the answer is "not fully," repent of it, ask His forgiveness, and give Him your all.

LISTEN TO HIS VOICE

תִּשְׁמָעוּ וּבְקֹלְוֹ

[THE HEBREW ROOTS
ARE SAMAH QOL]

To Listen, hearken, understand, be obedient to His Voice

"Listen to His voice" is an injunction that takes us beyond the written Word to the very voice of God. You may hear Him audibly, in a dream, or in a vision. When we meditate on these two Hebrew words, SAMAH QOL, we may think first of Isaiah's prophecy to the people of Zion who cry out to the Lord, *"The Lord will give you the bread of adversity and the water of affliction, but your Teacher will no longer hide Himself—with your own eyes you will see Him. And whether you turn to the right or to the left, your ears will hear this command behind you: "This is the way. Walk in it."* (Isaiah 30:20-21).

Hopefully, we will remember the incredible action of the Holy Spirit of God, the RUACH HaQODESH. The call to **listen** is a call to be in the Holy Spirit, to walk in the Spirit, pray in the Spirit, function in the Spirit, be sensitive all the day long to what our Lord and Father is saying to us. To be infused with the Spirit of God.

Remember the New Covenant prophesied by the Prophet Joel and later declared by the Apostle Peter:

> *'AND IT SHALL BE IN THE LAST DAYS,' God says,*
> *'THAT I WILL POUR OUT MY SPIRIT ON ALL MANKIND;*
> *AND YOUR SONS AND YOUR DAUGHTERS WILL PROPHESY,*
> *AND YOUR YOUNG MEN WILL SEE VISIONS,*
> *AND YOUR OLD MEN WILL HAVE DREAMS;*
> *AND EVEN ON MY MALE AND FEMALE SERVANTS*
> *I WILL POUR OUT MY SPIRIT*
> (Joel 2:28-29).

The call is to be fully aware that the God of the Universe wants to direct our paths in a most intimate way. God can use any method to reveal His specific will to an individual, whether by His written word, divinely directed desire, illumination, revelation, vision, or dream. It may be by way of *"an inspired Word birthed within your own spirit, a whisper from the Holy Spirit like the still, small voice that spoke to Elijah in the cave. It is a divinely inspired impression upon your soul, a flash of thought or a creative idea from God. It is conceived in your spirit but birthed into your natural understanding by divine illumination.*" (Bill Hamon. *Prophets and Personal Prophecy: God's Prophetic Voice Today*, 1987).

We need to be sensitive throughout each day and in the night that the Spirit of God wants to break into our consciousness and speak His word. Remember that Jesus said it was a good thing that He was going to the Father since the Holy Spirit would come in His stead to both comfort and guide us!

SWEAR BY HIS NAME

DEUTERONOMY 10:20

וּבִשְׁמוֹ תִּשָּׁבֵעַ

[V'SHEMO TSHAVAH]

Swear by His Name; see Gen 21:23, Matt. 5:34, James 5:12

The injunction to "Swear by His Name" occurs only one time in our eight occurrences. It is a bit startling since both Jesus and the Apostle James appear to specifically forbid making oaths. The imperative verb tSHA-VAH (swear) first occurs in the Hebrew scriptures in Genesis 21:23 where Abimelech charged Abraham to *"swear by God"* that he would not deal falsely, and Abraham did so.

What are we to make of this? For Jesus said *"Again, you have heard that it was said to those of ancient times, 'You shall not swear falsely, but carry out the vows you have made to the Lord.' But I say to you, Do not swear at all, either by heaven, for it is the throne of God, or by the earth, for it is his footstool, or by Jerusalem, for it is the city of the great King. And do not swear by your head, for you cannot make one hair white or black. Let your word be 'Yes, Yes' or 'No, No'; anything more than this comes from the evil one."* (Matthew 5:33-37). Jesus does not specifically mention using Father's name as a backup to your promise, but it would appear to be prohibited as well.

Thoughtful Jews who lived in the first centuries after Jesus's birth also did not encourage oaths. In fact, the Babylonian Talmud that was codified between 200 and 500 AD records Rabbi Yossi ben Judah as saying: *"Let your "yes" be yes , let your "no" be no." (Bava Metziah* 49a). And Philo, an important Jewish philosopher of the first century also said, *"The bare word of a virtuous man should be like an oath, steadfast, inviolable, and true. Should necessity require an oath, let a man swear by his father and mother instead of by the name of the highest and first essence."* All of these anti-oath statements begs the question, What must the phrase "Swear in His Name" in Deuteronomy 10:20 truly mean if we take the words of Jesus, Yossi ben Judah, and Philo into account?

One perspective is that Jesus and His fellow righteous Jews took the honor of God's name very seriously. The *Babylonia Talmud* in *Shevuot 39a* tells us that the entire world shook when God issued the prohibition of swearing falsely. Even if one swears truthfully, there is a risk of too much familiarity and a lack of proper awe and respect for God, reminiscent of the sin of the people of Beit Shemesh which is 20 miles west of Jerusalem. Beit Shemesh was the first town encountered when the Ark of the Covenant was being returned to Israel. Many people there were struck down because they had looked into the Ark.

It seems it would certainly be wrong to swear in the Name of God for private purposes, that is, not for God's purposes. You would be using God's name like it was yours to control. But by definition, you cannot control God. There must a time when swearing by God's name is appropriate (think Paul on his last visit to Jerusalem); all the clear restraint cited by the sources is evidence that God's name was likely being abused terribly in the first century as a matter of course.

The *Talmud* as codified in the *Shulchan Aruch* (literally "Set Table") is the most widely accepted code of Jewish law ever written. Compiled in the 16th century by Rabbi Joseph Karo, it describes a lengthy warning to anyone who swears:

We say to him that the entire world shook when Hashem said, "Thou shalt not take My name in vain" . . . Regarding all other sins only the one who commits the sin is punished; for swearing falsely he and his entire family is punished . . . and the entire world is punished for this sin . . . One is punished immediately for this sin . . .

I hope never to be tempted to go beyond Jesus's instruction not to swear at all. But if I swear at all, may it be because God has called me to! And may it be so for you!

SUMMING UP

This review of eight important scriptures from the first six books in our Bible underscore at least seven relational aspects of walking closely with God. Each is different from the others. Sit with each one of these over and over in your times of meditation. Father has given us a different way of seeing the richness of His call to relate to Him. To avoid hopefully unnecessary distraction, we have dropped "Swear by Him" from our final list leaving us with seven special imperatives to deeply and seriously consider.

Love Him

Cleave to Him

Walk in His Ways

Keep His Commandments

Fear Him

Serve Him

Listen to His Voice

PRAYING THE IMPERATIVES

Many people use all seven imperatives as a prayer outline in their early morning and late-night prayer time and have found them to be true game-changers. There are several ways to get these imperatives fixed in your heart and mind. One is to declare them. In other words, confess that they are so: "I will love You, O Lord, with all my heart, my soul, my strength, and my mind. I will cling to You, I will lean toward You, I will cleave to You. I will walk in Your ways this day." And so forth.

Another way is to petition the Father of the Universe to help you with all seven imperatives. When you do this, you may find that God will alert you as you pray to specific things that you need to see, pray about, desire, and do. You can pray through all seven in the morning and evening or go through only one imperative each day. For maximum impact, it probably is best to do all seven during each prayer time.

Don't rush. It can take twenty to thirty minutes to pray through the seven imperatives depending on how fast you go. And listen. Each day, you can increase your awareness of God and His intentions for you.

One last tip, follow the injunction from Psalm 100:4: "Enter into His gates with thanksgiving and His courts with praise; be thankful to Him and bless His name!" The best way to start our prayers is through thanksgiving and praise.

PRAYER SEQUENCE #1

"LOVE GOD WITH ALL YOUR HEART, SOUL, STRENGTH, AND MIND."

And your Neighbor as Yourself!

The first imperative is what Jesus said was the most important thing that God wants for each one of us. It is a great gift if we can actually receive it and be transformed by it. Some of us start our prayer in the middle of the night by expressing our great yearning to truly LOVE GOD with all our heart, soul (that is, your complete being), strength, and mind. However, we are not simply stating those yearnings to Father. We are petitioning Him for help because we recognize within ourselves that our love for Him is weak, underdeveloped, and in need of expansion.

Those four zones (heart, soul, strength, mind) become four separate petitions. We reflect on our hearts for God and acknowledge our need for a deeper and more expansive heart. God has been with each one of us since our beginning, with a deep desire for our wellbeing. The love in our hearts deepens as we consider His love and affection.

Our second consideration is our whole being (the Hebrew word NEPHESH encompasses our entire being—flesh and spirit) and our longing for our souls to be completely in love with the Godhead—Father, Son, and Holy Spirit.

Next, we humbly ask for Father's help with our limited strength, so that we may not waver or faint out of weakness but rather rise and let our strength be given over to our God. "My flesh and my heart faileth; But God is the strength of my heart and my portion forever." (Psalm 73:26).

Finally, we consider our minds and their need to know more about God and the things of God. We pray that we will dive deeper into the Scriptures and understand more about the wonder and beauty of God.

These four divisions of our being (heart, soul, strength, and mind) also affect how we treat others, and we can offer similar petitions for those close to us as well as those more distant.

Every day is an opportunity to learn more about our Creator and those with whom we are connected. Each time you pray this overarching imperative to LOVE, you will catch new dimensions of your need for a deeper and more pure love.

PRAYER SEQUENCE #2

"CLEAVE TO GOD"
Deuteronomy 10:12-13

Cling to Him! Cleave to Him! Lean into Him! How deeply we yearn to unite our very being to God. We know that the day ahead may bring dangers that can unravel rather than tighten our bond to God, and we need help from the One who made all that exists! We don't want anything to come between us and our Heavenly Father. Our second entreaty is to remain firmly connected—consciously drawing close to God through the day.

Some days, you will be aware of new threats as you pray for closeness. Or, you may envision a new form of bonding. Your mind's eye might conjure imagery from Renaissance paintings depicting the Lord's Supper, where the beloved disciple, John, is *leaning* toward Jesus. That image can ignite a desire to *lean* toward Jesus all day—to incline toward him—as you increasingly cling to God. If forces of evil attempt to draw you closer, you can lean even more resolutely into God's embrace!

The Last Supper by Jan Erasmus Quellinus

PRAYER SEQUENCE #3

"WALK IN HIS WAYS"
Deuteronomy 10:12-13

Yes, we want to "walk in His ways," but, we need help! The third imperative, to walk in God's ways, reminds us of God's revelation to Moses on Mount Sinai, as recorded in Exodus 34:6-7. Remember, Moses had asked God who He was—what were His ways. And the God of the Universe answered him while He sheltered Moses in the mountain's crevice.

Familiarizing ourselves with the essence of these two verses in Exodus 34:6-7 is a blessing. It allows us to envision a metaphorical scroll unfolding before our inner eyes, revealing God's ways in the same sequence that they were disclosed to Moses. The summary sequence from Exodus follows:

1. Compassionate

2. Gracious

3. Slow to Anger

4. Abounding in Steadfast Covenantal Love

5. Abounding in Truth

6. Maintaining Steadfast Love generationally

7. Forgiving the Most Serious Sins

8. But Allowing Consequences to Stand for a Season

During your time of prayer, contemplate each one of these aspects of God's ways. Pray that you will walk in a similar manner when interacting with others. Each of these attributes is entirely relational. As you pray, specific individuals may come to mind that need your loving action or response. Pray that your attitude and action will express God's pattern.

PRAYER SEQUENCE #4

"KEEP HIS COMMANDMENTS"
Deuteronomy 10:12-13

As we plunge further into this pool of prayer, the awareness of our need for help increases with each plea. "Keep His Commandments" encompasses not only our external actions but also our inner being. "Lord, help us comprehend and live in line with Your commandments!"

The Bible is chock-full of instructions–God's Operating Instructions for Human Beings. While many are familiar with the Ten Commandments, many other commandments go unnoticed, such as the one expressed in Leviticus 19:28 or Jesus's teachings in Matthew 5:28. God gives us instructions for our long-term benefit. Immerse yourself in the Scriptures every day, be alert to His instructions, pray that you may have the will to keep His commandments. While you are praying, it is entirely possible that our merciful Lord will impress upon your heart specific commands tailored to your unique circumstances.

PRAYER SEQUENCE #5

"FEAR HIM"
Deuteronomy 10:12-13

Yes, we want to have more than a healthy respect for God. He transcends our understanding and surpasses everything that exists. God's power is immense, and His nature remains partially veiled to us.

Take a moment to reflect on the grandeur and might of our Creator. Pray for a heightened awareness of His magnificence; allow it to permeate your being. Echo the exclamation of our Hebrew ancestors, proclaiming, "GADOL ELOHAI"— Great is our God!

We desire to be consumed by profound awe and the utmost reverence. Yet, are we? "Lord, help us be filled with true awe and reverence this day, for You are worthy of all praise and adoration!"

PRAYER SEQUENCE #6

"SERVE HIM"
Deuteronomy 10:20

At this moment in your prayers, Father should have your undivided attention! What can you do to express your love and affection? "I *DO* want to serve You—I *DO* want to serve Your people—I *DO* want to serve Your creation." When you approach Almighty God with a request for opportunities to serve, be attentive. It could be through acts of kindness towards strangers on the street, assisting your friends, supporting your coworkers, nurturing your child, or cherishing your spouse. Remember the profound words of Matthew 25:40-45: "As you have done it do the least of these, you have done it to Me."

> *"SERVE the Lord with gladness;*
> *Come before Him with Joyful Singing.*
> *Know that the LORD is God.*
> *He has made us, and we are His.*

The LORD is good.
His Steadfast Love endures forever,
And His Faithfulness to all generations."
(adapted from Psalm 100)

PRAYER SEQUENCE #7

"LISTEN TO HIS VOICE"
Deuteronomy 13:4

Lord, I humbly come before You, seeking your divine guidance and presence. Grant me the wisdom and discernment to be ever alert to the messages You may be conveying to me. Open my heart and mind to receive Your words and understand Your will.

In your infinite wisdom, You have provided us with Your most holy scripture, a treasure trove of timeless wisdom and guidance. I ask that You speak to me through the sacred texts, illuminating passages that are relevant to my current situation and offering me insights and clarity.

I want to be open to receiving messages through dreams and visions, as You have spoken to Your servants throughout history in such extraordinary ways. I pray that You grant me dreams that are filled with symbolism and meaning from You, helping me to decipher the messages You intend to convey.

As I navigate through the various circumstances of my life, I beseech You to speak to me through them. Help me recognize the patterns and coincidences that should serve as signposts on my journey. Enable me to discern Your voice amidst challenges, so that I may make choices aligned with Your divine purpose.

Lord, I know You often choose to speak through the people You place in my life. Whether it be a friend, an acquaintance, or even a stranger, I pray that You will use their words, insights, and advice as vessels for Your message. Give me the humility to listen attentively and the discernment to filter out what is true and beneficial.

Help me listen with an open heart and a receptive spirit. Grant me the patience and perseverance to wait for Your answer, whether it comes immediately or unfolds over time.

May Your voice be the guiding light that directs my steps and shapes my decisions. Help me to align my will with Yours for I know that You have my best interests at heart. In all things, may I glorify You and live according to Your purposes. LORD, what are You speaking to me?

LOVE HIM

CLEAVE TO HIM

WALK IN HIS WAYS

KEEP HIS COMMANDMENTS

FEAR HIM

SERVE HIM

LISTEN TO HIS VOICE

(See Deuteronomy 13:4)

BIBLIOGRAPHY

Babylonia Talmud, Shevuot 39a, Sefaria.com, 2022, Internet.

Genenius. *Hebrew and Chaldee Lexicon to the Old Testament Scriptures*, Wiley, New York, 1893, Print.

Hamon. *Prophets and Personal Prophecy: God's Prophetic Voice Today,* Destiny Image, Shippensburg, 1987, Print.

Irenaeus. *Irenaeus on the Christian Faith*, condensed by James R. Payton, Jr., Cambridge, James Clark & Co., 2012, Print.

Irenaeus. *The Ante-Nicene Fathers, Vol. 1*, Against Heresies, translated by Roberts and Rambaut, Buffalo, The Christian Literature Company, 1885, Print

Karo, Rabbi Joseph. *Shulchan Aruch*, Venice, 1565 original, *https://www.koltorah.org/halachah/shevuot-in-beit-din-civil-courts-and-daily-life-part-one-by-rabbi-chaim-jachter,* 2022, Internet.

Lewis, C. S. *Out of the Silent Planet*, New York, Harper Trophy, 2000, Print.

Lewis, C. S. *The Lion, The Witch and the Wardrobe*, New York, Scribner, 2003, Print.

Luzzato, *Mesillas Yesharim*, Rahway, New Jersey, Mesorah Publications, 2020, Print.

Maimonides, Moses. *A Maimonides Reader*, edited by Isadore Twersky, Springfield, Behrman, 1972, Kindle.

Maimonides, Moses. *The Guide for the Perplexed*, translated by M. Friedlander, Ph.D, Dover Publications, New York, 1956, Print.

Maimonides, Moses. *Rambam, Mishneh Torah*, Yad Hachazakah, annotated & translated by Avraham Finkel, Scranton, Yeshivah Beth Moshe, 2001, Print.

Moses. *The Book of Exodus*, Vol. 1 & 2, edited by Rabbi Rosenberg, New York, Judaica Press, 1997, Print.

Moses. *The Living Torah*, translated by Rabbi Aryeh Kaplan, Jerusalem, Maznaum Publishing Corp, 1981, Print.

The Jewish Encyclopedia, Vol IX, Isidore Singer, Editor, Funk and Wagnalls, New York, 1925, Print.

The Jerusalem Bible, Catholic translation, London, Darton, Longman & Todd, 1966, Print.

Rashi. *Commentary on Jeremiah*, translated by Freedman, England, Soncino Press, Print.

Snaith, Norman. The Distinctive Ideas of the Old Testament, New York, Schocken Books, 1975, Print.

Theological Dictionary of the Old Testament, Vol I & V, edited by Botterweck & Ringren, translated by D. Green, Grand Rapids, Eerdmans, 1986, Print.

Yonah, *Shaarei Teshuvah – The Gates of Repentence*, Rahway, New Jersey, Mesorah Publications, 2021, print.